PRED

Men

DAVE HILL

PHŒNIX

A PHOENIX PAPERBACK

First published in Great Britain in 1997 by
Phoenix, a division of the Orion Publishing Group Ltd
Orion House
5 Upper Saint Martin's Lane
London, WC2H 9EA

A CIP catalogue record for this book is available
from the British Library.

ISBN 0 297 84110 6

Typeset by SetSystems Ltd, Saffron Walden
Set in 9/14 Stone Serif
Printed in Great Britain by
Clays Ltd, St Ives plc.

Women are inclined to complain that men are all the same, and only the most myopic of men cannot see at least a little of what those women mean. But that doesn't mean it's true. Conceded, many men are indolent, idiotic and infantile. Agreed, far too many are desperate, dangerous and out of self-control. Yet, while womankind may be entitled to the consolations of over-simplification, it is also true that the men of the Western world are probably less 'all the same' at this millennial moment than they have ever been.

There are many reasons for this. The pleasing irony is that women themselves are one of the biggest. New technology, massive shifts in patterns of employment, changes in the structures of families and the voraciousness of consumerism have all played crucial parts in separating men from former certainties, releasing them from old conventions, and generating both the choice and the obligation to diversify. But it was the women's movement, its polemicists, scholars and everyday adherents, who began making really big cracks in the old moulds of masculinity, to challenge the enduring myths of manhood with different stories of their own.

There is an important sense, then, in which the future of men began thirty years ago, because in excavating their own pasts from the footnotes of 'his story' women also wrote a new history of men. Much of it was most unflattering to its subject, and some was very ugly to behold. Yet its enormous implications will reach deep into tomorrow, not the least of which is that in seeking to liberate women it has also handed men the tools with which to liberate themselves.

We should all hope men will use them. The future of men depends fundamentally on their own and the wider society's willingness to learn from the ways in which masculinity has been defined and constructed, used and misused in the past: a brave and imaginative appraisal will help make men's futures brighter and those of women and children too; a sullen, defensive refusal to do so may gratify some men but consign others to bleak underfulfilment and much worse. The positive approach is essential: the modern world is changing fast and in ways which are rendering some of the old models of masculinity marginal if not redundant. For three decades women have been making most of the running. Men need to get up to speed.

Rapid change gives rise to high hopes and great anxieties all at once. Fifty years ago everybody knew what a man was meant to be: protector, provider, paragon of permanence. He didn't always make the grade but at least everyone knew the pass mark. Now as the next chapters in humanity's story begin to unfold, many men are wondering where they fit in to the narrative. They have good reason: the momentum of the age will not propel all of them in the same direction. Rather, it will affect them differentially, varying according to their social class and circumstances as well as being welcomed or otherwise according to their personal taste. There will be no definitive Millennium Man. There will be several. Some will be truly marvellous. Others will make the rest of us wish they had not been born.

So far, and speaking very generally, there have been two sorts of reaction to the shifting terrain. One welcomes it for raising the possibility of men kicking some of their most destructive and self-destructive habits: patriarchal aggression, emotional isolation, permanent puerility and other characteristics which are often reinforced by the expectations of fellow men and, to some extent, by those of women. It anticipates men being less separate from women, sharing greater common ground. It welcomes the attempts by some men to be more emotionally receptive and looks forward to the further slackening of rigid definitions of how a 'real' man should be.

Others are alarmed. In his famous book *Iron John*, the poet Robert Bly invokes ancient myths to argue that modern men have lost touch with an essential part of themselves. The *Iron John* story tells of a Wild Man, long buried, who is brought up from under water, and the need of a young boy to find the courage to release him from his cage, thereby confronting a core part of himself. In *The Sibling Society* Bly complains that the collapse of patriarchal structures has led to disrespect and chaos. He describes 'the Woodstock moment' in which the young broke with tradition, and how nothing has been quite right since. The loss of male authority also worries Louis Farrakhan, leader of the illiberal black separatist organization the Nation of Islam. His Million Man March on Washington irritated many women, black women included, but it also won support because it engaged with a malaise which has seen too many black Americans entering the criminal justice system and too many failing to fulfil their duties to their partners and children. The March was a protest to the government. But it was also a call for a return to the traditional model of masculine command of family and home.

In Britain, something similar animates at least some elements in the network of campaigners agitating for the enhancement of what they call 'fathers' rights'. Detectable in the rhetoric of the pressure group Families Need Fathers is the complaint that modern mothers deserve much of the blame for the collapse of families. Their literature dedicates unhealthy amounts of space to tips on how to outmanoeuvre the women they've learned to hate. Much of their crusading zeal seems to derive from the belief that feminism has 'gone too far'. There is a Canute-like quality to all these arguments. Yet they harmonize with a common cry against history's crashing tides. It is a similar cry to that heard from those frantic to discredit revelations about men's sexual abuse of children, to demean women complainants in high-profile legal actions over sexual harassment or to denounce lesbian motherhood. And although their positions are ultimately untenable, they have acquired legitimacy because they seem to provide solutions to what many believe is a crisis of male identity in the West.

This may be no exaggeration. An edifice of data is not required to detect the unwillingness or inability of men to adapt or to behave in a well-balanced way. Prised out of their easy chairs in front of the fire, they are unable to get comfortable elsewhere. That's just the nice ones: most people, including most men, have to live every day with the bullying boss, the hostile driver, the swaggering youth prowling the street. And men are miserable, too: the incidence of male suicide has increased by 70 per cent in the last dozen years. The very processes which offer men the prospect of some new kinds of freedom have brought others nothing but disintegration and despair. Men have secured permission to deviate significantly from at least some of the conventional models for being male, but not all those deviations are desired, especially among those for whom conformity means security.

And men are mysterious. In a curious way, their long-held control of the human narrative has meant that big parts of their lives have been taken for granted. And because men are habitually reticent about themselves, you can't always be certain what they're like. Their appearances can be deceptive. The external Bruce Springsteen may mask the Homer Simpson within. The man who goes emotionally AWOL into private worlds of televised sport and garden sheds may flourish when in company, telling jokes, flirting, singing and telling the same jokes all over again. The man who never cleans the bathroom sink may also be the man who hoovers compulsively when he gets in from work and becomes hopelessly unsettled by a half-full litter bin. The man who makes assiduous selections from his wardrobe every morning might actually prefer to wear the garments in his wife's. The man who drinks and fights and gets arrested may also be the man who cries alone. Some men solicit brief sexual encounters with women, some do the same with other men, and some seek no kind of sexual encounters at all. Some men ignore, humiliate and even cruelly misuse their children. Others collect their children from school, cook their dinners, kiss their eyes and sing them off to sleep. Men can be any of these things, and sometimes two or three at once.

Men are not always everything we'd wish. But they are extremely various, and it's important to appreciate this when trying to predict their future. Even to acknowledge it is the start of taking issue with the stubborn and destructive belief that there is such a thing as an essential male identity, an unchanging masculine dimension of a natural human order from which it is unwise, if not downright dangerous, for any to deviate. For men have always deviated and will go on doing so. The great unknown about men's future is not whether it will be different from the past, but whether they themselves will improve.

In the next century men will experience a range of new and different relationships with the world of remunerative work. The silicon chip is replacing the old steel wheels of industry, and nothing is more certain than that this profound transformation in the technology of production will continue – except, perhaps, that its blessings for men will go on being mixed.

Some will find its consequences liberating because, whether by accident or design, it will result in them striking a better balance between their work and their domestic lives: between making a living and making a life with the people they love most and doing their full share of the housework. Many of the tensions which tear families apart arise from the imbalance between these two key spheres of existence: men work for too many hours and have too little time or energy for their partners or their children; their partners resent it, their children regret it; everybody suffers as a result. But those who are able to find an accommodation between making money and doing domestic labour will often feel far better for embarking on the voyage of discovery into the formerly alien female universe of kitchen grime and ground-in dirt, of grubby toddlers and grumbling teenagers. The transformation, already under way, may never be more than partial in the majority of cases. At present, even in households where both partners earn the main burden of domestic work, manual, managerial and the care of children, is still carried by women. Metaphorically, and sometimes literally, men still do not know how to operate the washing machine. But at least they have discovered where it is.

Those who figure out what all the different buttons do *and* learn the fine art of pairing socks will be in the vanguard of masculine change. For centuries the work a man does for a living has defined his identity, the way he describes himself to others: men are binmen or barristers first, partners and fathers second. Many are work obsessives, archetypally unable to leave the office psychologically even when they are physically somewhere else (and that is often how their bosses like it). For others their work anchors the soul of entire communities: farming in rural France, fishing in Scandinavia, car production in Detroit, coal mining and steel production in parts of Britain and Germany, but many of these have shrivelled into shadows of their former selves. Meanwhile, lighter industries and the service sector have ballooned. The keyboard operative with clean fingernails is now more numerous than the horny-handed son of toil. And, of course, 'he' may very easily be a 'she'.

These and other trends in the organization, availability and nature of work are set to continue for as far ahead as any economist can see. The 'feminization' and fragmentation of the labour market will continue apace, with many more jobs disappearing and a large proportion of the new ones created being part-time and taken by women. Though still far from enjoying equal power and status, women have made huge incursions, in the professions, in business, in the public sector and on the shop floor. The non-domestic workplace will cease to be the male stronghold it once was. In Britain more than half the workforce will be female by the year 2005. Most damagingly for men, the high and largely stable levels of male employment which many industrialized nations took for granted in the first three decades after the war are unlikely to return. America has its welfare 'underclass' and for all the 'tough love' Bill Clinton has mustered, nothing looks likely to shift it. In Western Europe job prospects depend crucially on the timing and form of the proposed 'monetary union' of national currencies and how much austerity individual national leaders are prepared to subject their people to in order to achieve it. Enthusiasts insist that it will all be for the best. But the expression 'full employment' has disappeared from political discourse.

We are all 'flexible' now, as many men once accustomed to certainty will continue to learn the hard way. Plenty have adapted – have *had* to adapt – but others, more set in their ways, cannot cope either with being 'stuck at home' or with the thought of doing 'women's work', whether in the kitchen or in the local electronics assembly plant. Until the mid-1970s nearly all men went outside the home to work and did so for pretty regular hours with optional overtime. But in Britain today, where flexibility is almost religiously cited as a virtue, a third of men who work outside the home routinely do so for more than fifty hours a week. Then there are those who work for very few and/or very unsocial hours, and still others who become well acquainted with the daytime television schedules because they cannot obtain paid work at all. Men of every sort have been sucked in to this void: not just the under-educated and unskilled, but middle-aged middle managers and young graduates denied the chance of independence, unable to fly the family nest, indulged by sometimes hard-pressed parents and finding even quite modest ambitions thwarted.

The forces which have stitched this patchwork of male experience are still in their relative infancy. It seems depressingly probable, then, that many men who are prosperous will go on finding it hard to enjoy the freedoms which prosperity is supposed to provide even if they find their jobs fulfilling: oppressed by overwork, fearing for their grip on financial rewards or of going without the pleasures of professional kudos, they will remain under-engaged with the people closest to them, the ones best fitted to provide sustenance for their half-starved inner selves. Then there are those who are not affluent but who do well enough materially: many of these will go on getting by but more fretfully, more menaced by the threat of unemployment or self-employed ruin.

As for those at the bottom of the heap, the permanently casualized, they seem destined to remain there, spread across a spectrum of social exclusion which has insanity at one extreme and career criminality at the other, many a persistent and intractable menace to each other and the communities in which they live. The police have long been sick of them, the courts clogged with them, the hospitals full of them on Saturday nights. There hasn't been so much worry about young working-class males for a hundred years, and there is no sign of it abating. Ten, twenty, thirty years from now all this will still be true. And the longer it goes on, the more complete will be the detachment of such men from any sense of the greater good and the more absolute will be their separation from the rest of society. This will confirm the already prevailing perception of them as irrevocably mad and bad, as creatures from a blighted netherworld, as a virtual subspecies whose very existence propagates dread.

But there will be a benign counterpart to the future tyranny of the labour market, and it will encourage the long-overdue reintegration of work and home in the lives of men. It is easy to forget that the rigorous separation of the two is relatively recent. It established itself as the norm only during the second half of the nineteenth century, a profound consequence of the industrial revolution. Rural and feudal societies became urban and capitalist ones, sometimes with extraordinary speed. The more it became established, the more the factory age imposed a rigid separation between the workplace and the home and between men and the women and children they shared it with.

The dichotomy of men as hunter-gatherers and women as child-bearers and home-makers was, of course, millennia old, but industrialization imposed a far sharper demarcation. Previously the ordinary man had tended to work on the same piece of rented land he lived on. This in itself kept him in closer physical proximity to the rest of his immediate family, and both he and his wife contributed to the common cause of supporting themselves from their crops, livestock or saleable skills, running their home and caring for their brood. Fathers played a central role in educating their children, passing on skills and knowledge, particularly to their sons. But waged labour took men away from the home every day for long stretches. In 1750 the average number of hours toiled each week had been forty-eight. Yet by 1900 it was regarded as a victory for organized labour that the working week had been reduced to around fifty-five hours including a Saturday half-day off.

Meanwhile, the home became more matricentral with women speaking for the first time of '*my* kitchen' or '*my* hearth', and children increasingly being taught in schools. Men became disengaged from chores and parenting, the more earnest self-improvers redirecting their energies towards relieving their womenfolk of these duties too. Mr Pooter, the fictitious keeper of *The Diary of a Nobody*, epitomized those 'superior clerks' employed by banks or insurance companies who were pleased to pay a live-in nanny and who would 'shrink from letting their wives do household work'. Plenty of women subscribed to this patriarchal configuration, a template of gentility on which the separate roles of men and women were clearly marked.

It has proved to be enormously enduring, surviving two world wars and a slump and emerging just as strong on the other side. Today, many look back and long for that ideal Fifties man. You knew where you were with him, and he seemed to know where he was with himself. He was the chap who came home to his wife from work at half-past five, looking forward to his tea. In Britain he was the solid fellow who bought his family's first television set in 1953 so all could gather round and watch the coronation of the Queen: he may even have helped with the washing up once the sponge cake had been eaten. Fifties man accumulated refrigerators and radiograms and allocated housekeeping money. He was the most stable fixed component of the nuclear family, a unit whose rules were plain and absolute. Marriage was the road everyone walked down, divorce was the dark end of the street. A wife was a woman who worked in the home and looked after the children. A husband was a man who went out and earned the money to support them. As a father he was kindly, firm and frequently peripheral. He romped with his children before bedtime, and may sometimes have smacked their behinds. But he left the rest to mother, who knew best.

That's the received wisdom and it survives partly because there is some truth in it, partly because the picture it paints of simpler times contrasts so completely with the uncertainties of the present. All nations have their version of it. John Major, Britain's prime minister throughout most of the 1990s, understood his country's very well. He often sought electoral comfort in the story of his own father, 'that proud stubborn man I loved'. Major told these stories well, eulogizing a steady striver trying to make a success of his garden-ornament business in a south London suburb, not only for his own sake, but for his family and, in some instinctive way, for his country too: a persuasive vision of the Eternal Nation, a place where many people would still rather like to live.

They are going to be out of luck, though. The gross imbalance of power between the sexes on which this (often illusory) image of stability was based has already begun to be corrected. Despite the fact that it is still women rather than men who know the contents of the freezer, the whereabouts of the gas bill and the names of the children's five best friends, the female doormat, the woman who 'waited on her husband hand and foot', is no longer commonplace. The day is approaching when she is more likely to provide the household with income than he is. But maybe he will have found his compensations in the kitchen, in the supermarket or at the school gate. Who knows: he may even be a fully rounded human being.

There is, though, widespread disquiet forecast on the domestic front. The die is already cast. Among European Community countries, divorce rates vary often in accordance with religious, cultural or legal particularities, but the general trend is up. In Britain it has spiralled, as it has in the United States, fuelling a broader and often vexed debate about the institution of the family and its distressing tendency to fall apart. The future of men depends a great deal on which side of the argument prevails.

For some, the urge to put Humpty back together again will remain strong, no matter how rotten an egg he is shown to have been. At its most extreme this will be expressed by those who advocate that divorce be made more difficult and that women should be wrenched out of work and education and put back in the home so that men can reclaim their rightful place at the head of the 'natural' family order. Fundamentalists always flourish during periods of flux, and their arguments will continue to be heard for as long as any faith remains in the fantasy family of yesterday. But, quite apart from the niceties of gender equality and social justice, it is a completely impractical position: take women out of the workplace and economies will crumble; and you can't uneducate the educated.

There will, though, be subtler overtures made to the regressive instincts of men and women alike. During the 1997 British general election campaign the Conservative Party's 'big idea' was to promise that if one parent gave up work in order to care for a new baby then their personal tax allowance would be transferred to their spouse. This would only have applied to married couples and, because it is almost always the woman who gives up work after a baby is born, was plainly intended to reassert the Tories' claim to being the guardians of 'traditional' family life. It did them no good at the ballot box. But that does not mean that similar 'messages' won't hold an attraction for politicians of whatever party again. It is worth recalling that the Labour Party too has had pretensions to being the champion of family orthodoxy. Some months before the 1997 election Peter Mandelson MP, one of Labour Leader Tony Blair's most trusted lieutenants, floated the idea of the state providing couples with a repayable 'dowry' after they were married to help them through any early financial difficulties.

This was clearly intended to be an incentive for couples to marry rather than cohabit and as such a blatant attempt at stealing the Tories' traditionalist clothes. However, Mandelson's kite did not fly into Labour's manifesto, and in practice policymakers seem quietly to have accepted that couples will continue to crumble at their present alarming rate and that tightening divorce laws does not lessen the incidence of misery or desertion. Life just isn't like that. Both the form and the content of heterosexual partnerships are set to keep moving away from the old models and people will come to accept this. For all the sound and fury of the Moral Majority in the United States and their kindred spirits elsewhere, the political and economic ascendancy of the right during the 1980s was not accompanied by a renewed embrace of stiff social attitudes. On the contrary, the hot air of implausible rhetoric may simply have helped to deepen scepticism about the idealization of conventional families. It certainly did not suppress the growing awareness that externally 'model' nuclear units could be cauldrons of terror and grief as well as crucibles of love. Family life has always been problematic. The difference in the future is that no one will pretend it isn't.

The tumultuous debate about marriage and the family engulfs all and sundry. But it has increasingly centred upon the conduct of the men within them. Initially this was due to the determination of women's rights campaigners to bring the full and appalling facts of domestic violence against women into the open, battery and rape alike. Their successes have been significant, not least in persuading the police to take criminal assault within the home more seriously, and in so doing bringing it more into the public domain. The same result will eventually arise from more recent, equally disturbing revelations about some 'family men' in their role as fathers.

The proverbial visiting Martian would be astonished to learn that the term 'father-figure' denotes paternalistic reliability and wisdom. The most shattering blow to this cherished image of fathers as benign patriarchs has been the inexorable exposure of the extent of child sexual abuse. Recent research suggests that 2 per cent of biological fathers have some amount of sexual contact with their children, usually their daughters. In about half these cases it is restricted to a single, isolated incident (though no less disturbing for that), but in one case in four the contact involves intercourse of cunnilingus. It is also thought that another 2 per cent or so of fathers behave towards their children in some non-contact sexualized way, such as verbal innuendo or exposure. The data on stepfathers is also alarming. At least one in eleven appears to have sexual contact with his stepdaughter before she is fourteen years old. (Nor is the sexual molestation of girls by men with whom they live or to whom they are related restricted to fathers and father-figures. Shere Hite's report on the American family found that '31 percent of girls and young women describe having had to deal with sexual abuse either from a father or step-father, a brother, an uncle or a grandfather.')

Society has yet to come to psychological grips with such devastating information. Court cases revealing the ruthlessness of predatory paedophiles have spread fears for the vulnerability of the young outside the home, yet the shockingly high incidence of ostensibly 'normal' men's sexual exploitation of their own children is proving much harder to face. Each revelation is greeted by panicked, vehement denial. Yet, despite the automatic deafness they inspire, these facts will slowly begin to be faced as more and more people – men and boys as well as women and girls – make their personal experiences public.

Unease about what some fathers do to their children will keep on growing, adding to the now unconcealed dismay over their increasing tendency to leave them. At least 1.6 million men in England and Wales today are the fathers of dependent children who live in other households. Typically, when parents split up it is the father who leaves the family home and the mother who continues to look after the children for the great bulk of the time. Recent surveys have shown that anything between 23 and 43 per cent of male divorcees with children lose touch with them completely after five years. The spread of such knowledge has had such an effect that social conservatives looking for convenient scapegoats to explain the crisis in the family are as likely to alight on absent fathers as they once were on single mothers on welfare. In Britain, this can be largely attributed to Conservative government ministers realizing that the welfare budget might be reduced if absent fathers were tracked down and made to pay towards their offsprings' keep. Even so, the reputation of fatherhood, once so sacrosanct, has suddenly fallen low.

Recovery will not be swift. But the need for it will concentrate minds on wider questions about fathers and what they are going to be for. It will mean addressing the potential for creating a new and higher standard of paternal conduct as part of an ongoing project dedicated to the replacement of the closed, patriarchal family with an open, democratized one which would do away with the nineteenth-century division of domestic labour along gender lines and the accompanying notion that fathers should be emotionally distant disciplinarians. It will encourage fathers to meet with both mothers and children on the common ground of parenting.

This work has already begun and it suggests that the outlook for fatherhood need not be all bleak. The welcome trend for men to be more involved in the processes of pregnancy and birth will also continue. The days when expectant fathers paced hospital corridors, smoking while their wives' howled in pain, are gone for ever and their incursion into delivery suites will not be reversed, even though they clutter up the place with camcorder equipment and get on midwives' nerves. Progress in other areas will continue too, albeit unevenly. Women quite literally carry the main load of pregnancy so maybe it is inevitable that even the most well-meaning men prepared to lie on the floor and practise panting with their spouses feel a bit out of place. Maternity units and clinics will struggle to become paternity units too. It won't be easy, but the spirit is certainly willing, which matters a great deal.

Social attitudes are changing fast. Twenty years from now the idea that women are comprehensively better equipped than men to care for children will seem quaint and anachronistic. At present it is still generally held that females are programmed to be more alive to the needs of children, but this piece of received faith will slowly be shaken as more and more men demonstrate – and discover for themselves – that it is not necessarily so. This is plain from the earliest stages. Men who take their newborns in their arms, as more and more do, are amazed at how very pleased those babies soon become to see them, how quickly they recognize their voices and imitate the ways they move their faces. Research has shown that this equality of sensitivity is apparent early in life. In one study, tapes of crying babies were played to boys and girls aged eight and fourteen. In terms of social responses, the girls exhibited more concern, but when concealed responses were measured, the boys' rising heart-rates and blood pressures showed that they were just as perturbed as the girls – typically male already, they just tried not to show it. Studies of adults have produced compatible outcomes. Left alone, men are no more or less clumsy at handling their babies than women, and they raise their voices to talk to them just as automatically. There are no absolute laws of nature in this game.

The lesson is simple: excluding a few very specific areas of expertise, most importantly the one which only people with breasts can master, men are perfectly capable of being as good – or as bad – at caring for children as women. It will make practical sense to learn it. The implications of doing so will go with the grain of changing employment patterns, the desire of women to enjoy childcare rather than endure it, and their patent wish that men would be less withdrawn and oafish. Even governments seem at least a little sympathetic: a guarantee of unpaid paternity leave is enshrined in the 'social chapter' of the Maastricht Treaty, which sets out employment rights in the European Community. Most importantly, it's what children want: one loving parent in the fabric of their lives is very nice; two is even better.

The principle that everyone benefits when fathers are closely involved with their children is certain to gain credence. It has been articulated most comprehensively by Adrienne Burgess, an Australian journalist based in Britain and a research fellow with the left-leaning Institute for Public Policy Research. The argument of her important book *Fatherhood Reclaimed* takes issue with both the traditionalist right and elements of the feminist left whose analysis proceeds from the belief that men have shown themselves unwilling and often unfit to take on parenting tasks and responsibilities. Burgess examines a body of under-reported data on fathers and concludes that, while it is regrettably true that many fathers do not participate very actively in the lives of their children, there are and always have been plenty who do and many who would welcome the chance to do more. She advocates measures to help bind fathers as closely to their children as mothers usually are, including the extension of 'family-friendly' employment practices, the creation of support service for fathers and the introduction of parenting education for boys and men.

If this project progresses in the new century it will help to liberate men, women and children alike from some of the family's most disfiguring failings. But success will be very far from automatic. The escalating imperatives of competitiveness will be difficult to square with even the demand of women for family-friendly workplaces, let alone the idea that men should benefit from them to an equal degree. A lot of women will also resist greater involvement by men, especially those many for whom parenting provides a space – perhaps the only space – within a family structure where they exercise power. Burgess believes that both men and women need to make cultural adjustments.

She also argues for changes in both the letter and the implementation of some parts of the Children Act (1989) as it relates to the care of children when their parents split up. The Act is regarded by most as a step forward because it is rooted in the principle that the child's interests should come first. However, rightly or wrongly, it does discriminate against the unmarried father, which, given the high levels of cohabitation and the ever more evident shortcoming of marriage as a stabilizing institution, seems an impractical response to modern realities. The Act denies him automatic parental responsibility, effectively a package of rights bestowed upon biological parents. He must apply to the mother to bestow it upon him, and if she refuses he will have to apply to the courts. Because the law wants the father to accept responsibility for his children, he is rarely denied. However, the process may be costly and is likely to exacerbate bad feeling.

The courts are also far more inclined to grant residence orders (formerly 'custody') to mothers than to fathers despite their insistence that there is no concealed bias. It is this which excites the considerable passions of fathers'-rights campaigners, who believe that fathers are done down by a confluence of the prejudices of reactionary judges and 'feminist'-influenced welfare officers. The fathers'-rights movement is generally rather silly – men don't need such a movement half as much as they need to grow up. And yet, almost despite itself, it advances one argument which will acquire greater force as the cause of promoting the involvement of fathers with their children gathers strength.

The Act provides for an outcome based on the concept of 'shared parenting', whereby any children from a broken relationship reside for roughly half of their lives in the respective homes of both parents rather than being based at just one, usually the mother's, and having limited 'contact' with their fathers (who were formerly granted 'access'). The courts rarely issue 'shared residence' orders, believing that children are better off having one home rather than two. They may do so more in the future because a growing body of evidence shows that children are not harmed by such arrangements (which some parted parents now make voluntarily). Indeed, for them it offers the enormous advantage of keeping them close to both their parents, which is what many children want: when parents fight it breaks their hearts; but losing one compounds the fracture and may mean it never heals.

There is an irony in the enthusiasm of the fathers'-rights movement for shared parenting: the angry dads rail against 'feminism' keeping them from their kids, but their insistence that men can be good 'mothers' is entirely consistent with mainstream feminist thought; it is more ironic still that the logic of this position could be taken to imply that families don't *necessarily* need fathers at all. Even the British courts now recognize that most lesbian couples make an excellent job of raising children.

Yet anticipating broader recognition that fathers aren't always essential is not the same as predicting that they will become redundant. The great majority of families will continue to contain one female parent and one male one who does not do terrible damage to his partner or his children. Fathers continue to be important figures in their children's lives and key members of families, however these are configured. Arguments about the rights and wrongs of that will continue. But even though the tides of history favour the progressive realists, there is one great imponderable and that is the matter of what men really want from family life. Do they mean it when they tell researchers that they long to dedicate more of their time and energy to domesticity and all the human complexities which thrive there? Or does the evidence of misdemeanour and desertion tell a more truthful tale? The hope for the future is that they will be both willing and able to make a better job of family life than before. The fear remains that they will not.

At the heart of the future of the family lies the matter of men's sexuality. Indeed, it lies at the heart of *any* question about the future of men. The subject is hugely fraught, and not simply because it is integral to the processes of procreation and the pursuit of sensual pleasure. Men's sexuality is highly politicized, its expression controlled and mediated by means of powerful cultural taboos.

When those taboos are broken, the fall-out can be ferocious, resonating far beyond the realm of the libido and raising terrors about the spread of disease, the maintenance of public order and even the integrity of national identities. The pressures on men to adopt the 'right' sexual mores and attitudes is immense, and has been tremendously harmful down the years. It has been used as a means of subjugating women, stigmatizing men who don't conform to those mores, and as a brutal weapon in the socialization of boys. Men are both the authors and the victims of a tyranny of sexual correctness which distorts personalities and blights millions of lives.

There is now a reasonable chance that this can change. The fact that male sexuality is considered worth discussing in an open and sometimes sensible way in the pages of magazines offers some sort of hope: a market for knowledge has been identified and will continue to expand. Once contemplated only with intense furtiveness, men's obsessive anxieties about their sexual selves have lately become loudly public. Today, it is impossible to walk up to a newsstand in any major town without Priapus poking you in the eye. But although there is something to be said for candour – it is a big improvement on embarrassment – will frankness contribute to maturity? Which way will the trouser worm turn?

Like so much else which has benefited men, the potential for a more enlightened male sexuality has been partly created by modern feminism, which has explored the dynamics of sexual repression, degradation and desire. This has not always enhanced the reputation of men, but it has helped them to make some remarkable discoveries: the clitoris, for instance. No longer does it nestle unnoticed among the footnotes of biology textbooks or cower in the corners of maidenly shame. It has taken centre-stage in today's non-stop carnal-knowledge cabaret and bids for equal billing with the penis. Men once knew little of it. But their relationship with it is now comparable to the one they have developed with the washing machine (see above).

Women have made the running in bringing men to their sexual senses from way back. Between the wars a number of factors, from the advent of tampons to the growing wish to control their own fertility, helped women overcome their own ignorance and prudishness. Birth-control pioneer Marie Stopes met a massive demand with her books *Wise Parenthood*, which argued the case for family planning, and *Married Love*, a guide to sex and marriage. A Christian manual for engaged couples called *The Threshold of Marriage* described the ways for both partners to reach orgasm and sold over half a million copies. Educated estimates also suggest that between the end of the First World War and the onset of the Second, the proportion of women who were virgins when they married fell from 80 to 60 per cent. If this was evidence of shopping around, they could hardly be blamed: the inter-war male was woeful at appreciating the needs of his female partner. A survey of working-class women found that only a third had ever achieved a sexual climax and only a minority claimed to derive any real pleasure from sex.

As well as expressing their wish to enjoy sex more, women have protested against men's misuse of their sexuality as an instrument of power. This has involved defining a few terms. The most emotive example is rape, and here the achievements of feminism are reflected in popular culture. In his 1972 movie *Play It Again Sam*, Woody Allen created a painfully funny portrayal of male sexual anxiety whose moral was that women were not impressed by the 'give 'em a good slap' machismo which Allen perceived Humphrey Bogart to have personified in the 1940s. Yet it contained a remarkably glib exchange between the Allen character and that played by his co-star Diane Keaton, who commented that her response to being raped would depend on who was doing the raping. The following year another romantic comedy (also scripted by male hands), *A Touch of Class*, had the redoubtable Glenda Jackson complaining that her lover George Segal's ill-timed spinal seizure had denied her her chance to be raped. These uses of the word reflected the idea that rape was the expression of unbridled male lust and might even be taken as a compliment. But feminism insisted that there was no relationship at all between male high sexual passion indulged with female consent and the act of misogynistic violence for which the word 'rape' should be reserved – and by the end of the 1970s it had ceased to be a suitable subject for jokes.

So now everyone knows that rape is bad and that men who fail to attend to the needs of their sexual partners are not very good in bed. This is all to the good. But, although men have been urged to travel down the road to enlightenment, it isn't clear that they've gone very far. Neither sexual assault nor the psychology which underpins it appears to be significantly less prevalent, if at all, despite the disapproval they now attract. And men, infinitely more than women, continue to use sexual slang to express hatred or heap humiliation. A 'wanker' is still an inadequate, symbolically someone who can't 'get a shag', even though research has shown that those men who have intercourse almost every day are also the ones who masturbate every two. It is still extremely common to hear the word 'cunt' used in a derogatory way and by males of every kind, from adolescent boys on street corners to senior editors on liberal newspapers. What does it say about men's sexual outlook when a vernacular term for the vagina doubles as a synonym for loathing and contempt?

Meanwhile, the welcome drive to improve erotic relations between the sexes often seems to have degenerated into an endless flap about 'performance', which is not the same thing as 'technique'. In 1972 Alex Comfort published *The Joy of Sex*, a candid but calm and humorous instruction manual for heterosexual love-makers which sold by the truckload and is back in print today. Dr Comfort's recurring theme was 'don't worry'. Where men were concerned this meant not fretting if they were unable to summon consecutive erections every night until dawn. Yet fret men still do, and how. Far from accepting with relief that there really is no male sexual gold standard, that men's bodies and libidinal predilections vary as much as women's taste in them, men seem to be tormenting themselves more relentlessly than ever with questions about the pertness of their pectorals, the tensility of their six-packs and, of course, that timeless favourite, the dimensions of their penises.

They will go on tormenting themselves, not least because some scientists fear that man's member is destined to shrink, much as those of several species from the animal kingdom are doing. But perhaps this latest mass palpitation is just a phase, a temporary retightening of the straitjacket of the past. After all, there has to be some sort of resistance to the prevailing trends of the last fifty years which have resounded with the noise of sexual barriers being broken.

Nothing else can explain the amazing effect of Elvis Presley – not just a musical sensation, but a sexual one too. Much was made at the time of the explicitness of the sexual signals his hillbilly body sent out, but there was more to it than brash bravado: after all, there was nothing very new about men making a spectacle of themselves. The chemistry, though, was different. Presley's persona was not that of a 'man's man' in the accepted sense (he was, in any case, a 'mama's boy'). His machismo was playful, self-mocking, and its startling overtness was complicated by an impression of sweet innocence about its effect. This qualification of his masculine persona was central to its charm, and consistent with the way he looked. Presley was, by the standards of his time, a contradiction in cultural terms: a working-class, redneck dandy. He wore the clothes of a hepcat, a vain, streetwise black man of a kind whose presumed sexual hunger and potency white America feared. But there was, too, a touch of fag-flash about him. Boyish and lean, he sculpted his hair into a crest at the front and wore it long, brushing his collar, at the back. He was pretty, vain and unrestrained. He was many things a proper man was not supposed to be, and, hallelujah, all the things that drove young women crazy. He made a difference. Even when he was whisked off to join the army it was plain that that difference was there to stay.

The possibility of sexual skittishness, tenderness and diversification which Presley suggested was not acknowledged by all who were excited by his music. There was little sign of it among the music's first British devotees. The typical Teddy Boy was a London tough in a mock-Edwardian drape suit with a quiff and enormous shoes: a thug in fop's clothing, outwardly outlandish, inwardly suspicious of a change in the weather. Nothing subversively feminine lurking within was likely to be nurtured. For Teds were still just men of their time with a craving for attention and an appetite for a fight. Women were things you jived with, tried to screw if you were sober (and failed to if you were not) and who ironed your parallel strides. Poofs were for punching, even though the Teds' style owed more than any of them would have cared to admit to the gay underground of the time.

That said, several sexual genies had escaped from the bottled-up past and there was no way of putting them back. The sexual meanings of the early male pop and rock stars varied in the minds of their inventors and beholders: the managers who invented the early boy pop bands were often gay svengalis, but there was nothing homosexual in the screams of their girl fans. When David Bowie came along, the ambiguous signals sent out became self-conscious: Bowie *knew* what he was doing when he wore a dress on his album covers or pretended to fellate the instrument of his guitarist. By the mid-1980s the British pop charts were regularly topped by 'gender benders' knowingly playing with the symbols of sexual 'otherness'. Gayness, or the appearance of it, went overground. When people saw a man in a frock they were shocked but not appalled, nor will they ever be again.

A feature of the future will be the fuller recognition of gay men's contribution to the Western way of life. Perhaps, too, there will be more appreciation that the 'out'-ward march of homosexuals, which no prohibitionist alive is ever going to reverse, has done an immense service to men of all orientations. Simply by refusing to be invisible, gays have taken issue with the fundamentals of 'official' manhood, a version of masculinity which has frequently been promoted at their direct expense but which has cruelly damaged other men too. By ostracizing, persecuting and just plain hating homosexuals, the state and the establishment have earnestly promoted and approved a highly restrictive model for true manhood designed to serve a far wider range of interests than just sexual conformity.

The borders of acceptable male sexuality became heavily guarded in the second half of the nineteenth century, and this was related to other organizational impulses of the time. Runaway change imposed social strains and the elites were concerned about their effect on the family unit, whose disjunction was seen as diminishing its former authority. A threat to order was identified, especially among young men, whose energies outside work hours were thought to need directing away from trade union activities or beer. The health and fitness of the male workforce also required attention in the interests of productivity and of military efficiency at a time of imperial expansion. There arose a strong desire to create channels for the expression of forms of masculinity which would address these grave concerns.

The most successful of these was sport. Most professional football clubs were founded at this time in the great cities and northern towns, often starting at parish level supported by patrician churchmen and the blooming crop of urban entrepreneurs, typically brewers. Beginning as outlets for athletic participation, it wasn't long before the stronger teams began attracting crowds, and in that way the roots of the football industry we all recognize today were sunk. The standard kick-off time of three o'clock was no accident: a football match was where the proletarian male went on Saturday afternoons after a morning at work and a grateful lunchtime in the pub. And like the workplace and the pub, football was a social zone from which women were almost totally absent. But sport was not only an avenue for recreation, it was also seen as a moral arena informed by the ethos of the English public schools.

The importance of these institutions to the development of sport and its role in shaping expectations of manhood is difficult to exaggerate. In Britain writers such as Thomas Hughes articulated the notion of Muscular Christianity, a cult of athleticism promoting cleanliness, godliness, heartiness and loyalty to (ironically) Queen and country. Honour on the playing field was prized more highly than any academic achievement. To earn it was to possess the proud essence of English manliness. A passage from Hughes' classic *Tom Brown's Schooldays* describing the captain of the football team, captures that spirit memorably: 'and over all is old Brooke, absolute as he [the leader] of Russia, but wisely and bravely ruling over willing and worshipful subjects, a true football king. His face is earnest and cheerful as he glances a last time over his array, but full of pluck and hope, the sort of look I hope to see in my general when I go out to fight.'

The joke that public schoolboys were (and are) the most fervent self- and mutual masturbators in the country now enjoys a wide constituency. But the ideology of sport reflected a terror of sexual nonconformity with all its overtones of secrecy, dirt and disease. A pivotal event in the history of male sexuality was the trial of Oscar Wilde in 1886, when Victorian homophobia reached its fevered climax. The brilliant Irish writer, wit and bon viveur was prosecuted under an amendment to the Criminal Law Amendment Act of 1885 which was actually designed to curb the purchase of young women for sexual services. Authored by the MP Henry Labouchère in a spirit of malicious mischief, the amendment outlawed all homosexual acts, and Wilde fell foul of it as

a result of his attempt to sue the Marquess of Queensberry, a dyspeptic homophobe whose son Lord Alfred
Douglas was Wilde's lover. Queensberry had written to
Wilde accusing him of 'posing as a sodomite'. The libel
case, unwisely brought, yielded damning details about
Wilde's sex life during his cross-examination. His sub-
sequent prosecution intensified a ferocious stigmatiza-
tion of 'the love that dare not speak its name' and helped
heighten paranoia about proclivities which offended per-
ceptions of what was defined as a 'healthy' and 'natural'
state of manhood.

This was sustained for decades after. Young men who
confessed to having homosexual feelings were advised by
their doctors to take more exercise. Some of the madder
commentators detected 'unnatural' leanings in the most
innocent matters of taste: woe betide the fellow who
forsook a sturdy pipe for the effeminate pleasures of
cigarettes, cared for his appearance or betrayed the slight-
est interest in home furnishings. In 1911 London courts
added injury to the insult of homosexual criminalization
by introducing birching as a punishment for male solici-
tation, supported by the Liberal Home Secretary and a
Conservative backbencher grumbling that 'people have
lost all sense . . . and all ideas of anything which makes a
man a man'.

The preoccupation with what 'makes a man a man' was
closely linked with a passion for imposing social obedi-
ence and order, and this was intensified by the rise of
militarism in Europe. The Edwardian years were strongly
characterized by the belief that national virility was

undermined by inappropriate forms of masculinity, and you couldn't be much more inappropriate than having sex with other men. As Britain made ready for war, the determination to uphold standards became greater. A collective male identity coalesced in the male psyche with the help of the *Boy's Own Paper*, the stories of Rider Haggart and newspaper accounts of Boer War battles. British men (widely supported by women) subscribed in massive numbers to the idea that patriotic warfare was a glorious adventure for the clean in mind and body, whose success might be contaminated by the enfeebling influence of 'nancy-boys' with their foul enthusiasm for buggery. In later years some observers argued that the failure of British manhood to resist the homosexual impulse contributed to the loss of the empire, and the fear that homosexuals were a threat to national security was scarcely assuaged by the discovery in 1951 that Foreign Office mandarins Guy Burgess, who was gay, and the bisexual Donald Maclean had for years been spying for the Soviet Union.

There was also a class dimension to the social policing of homosexuality. The elites often accepted them in their own ranks so long as their 'inversions' were kept out of sight of the *hoi polloi*: hence the toleration of extraordinary goings-on in the Guards regiments, whose members seem to have spent most of the Victorian era helping each other out of their uniforms with barely a word of rebuke. The same principle applied to other deviations: hence discreet coteries of well-bred fellows with a taste for the sting of the birch servicing an underground market in books with coded titles like *The Romance of Chastisement*. Difficulties arose when the secret lives of respectable figures became public. It was feared that such hot knowledge would put corrupting ideas into the lower orders' heads: firstly, that the establishment might be a pit of perverts; secondly, that they might practice a bit of perversion themselves. This explains the furore over Wilde. It would later inform official concern over the publication in 1948 of Alfred Kinsey's study *Sexual Behaviour in the Human Male*, which found that 37 per cent of the male population of North America had experienced homosexual orgasm and another 13 per cent had at some point been quite attracted to the idea.

The presence of homosexual potential among ostensibly totally 'straight' men is still something we don't talk about much. This is likely to change, especially after the inevitable triumph of gay campaigns for full and equal civil rights. Holland and Hawaii have both inched towards this in recent years, and the 'don't ask, don't tell' compromise reached between Bill Clinton and the American armed forces leaders over lesbian and gay service personnel is such a palpable absurdity that it cannot possibly last. Victory will be won on all fronts because the arguments against, already recognized as flimsy, will become untenable as liberal social attitudes become ever more securely ensconced in mainstream opinion. Gay weddings will be commonplace, even in churches. Public demonstrations of gay affection will increasingly go unremarked. Discrimination will linger, but its practitioners will appear Stone Age. Gay business is hugely lucrative, and where there is profit, there is acceptance. Once all this is in place and formal equality achieved, there will be less need for homosexuals to assert the validity of what is distinctive about them and more room in the sexual-political discourse for what they have in common with heterosexuals.

To everyone's surprise, there will be plenty. It will emerge that the futures of gay men and those of straights are going to be more closely entwined. Realizing and accepting this will do wonders for all but the most hidebound of heterosexual men because it will help them free themselves from their own sexual prisons, and women along with them. All the old absolutes, all the tired prescriptions, will finally be revealed as false and it will be increasingly accepted that there is no such thing as a pure masculine sexual identity; that heterosexual and homosexual are not polar opposites, the one 'normal', the other an offence against nature. Rather they are just starting points of reference on a variegated sexual map offering a range of routes to fulfilment.

One key life activity where men of differing sexualities are discovering a common interest is the one which has always seemed impossible in the past – parenting. Conservative thinkers opposing homosexuals achieving civil parity have sometimes pressed their case by saying that their inability to contribute to the reproduction of the human race disqualifies them. The whole foundation of that argument has now been rendered factually bogus. Gay men *do* have children, raise them with their partners in two-dad households and do it rather well. As yet there aren't all that many. Within ten years there will be plenty.

This is just one example of how developments in the technology and the morality of procreation are transforming the gender landscape. They will seriously qualify the pre-eminence presently accorded to biological links between adults and children when ascribing the status of 'parent'. They will have huge, diverse and complicated implications for the already tangled arguments over the balance of rights and responsibilities between mothers and fathers and those expecting or wishing to become so. They will throw into even deeper confusion what the very terms 'mother' and 'father' actually mean.

To begin at the very Beginning: in the Eden of the future things will be very different between Adam and Eve. She will feel no shame about the consequence of having listened to the serpent. He will have more power than God over the destiny of his seed. Just as women will regard sex as an activity inseparable from the pursuit of pleasure, so men will take a more central interest in the mechanics of impregnation.

The New Age of reproduction will have many benefits for men. For a start there will be no *coitus interruptus* in Paradise. At least, there will be no need to worry that it might be necessary. Within a few years, a hormonal contraceptive for men – a male Pill – will become commercially available and the evidence is that plenty will be ready to try it. It is frequently, and not unreasonably, argued that men will never be as reliable as women in taking the Pill. And yet researchers in this field have never been short of volunteers, and 95 per cent of participants ask if they can keep on taking the Pill (or injection) after the trial is over. The appeal is easy to see. It will offer all the benefits of the female Pill to both partners and, with the man doing the swallowing, the complications involved with accommodating the menstrual cycle will not arise. For the responsible man it'll be just another item on his list of daily ablutions.

Of course, the male Pill won't just be for settled hetero couples. It will be of interest to any man wishing to suppress his sperm for whatever reason. But even the man who likes the idea because he (recklessly) believes it will take the risk out of rogering any willing female who lingers on the back seat of his car will find his perspective on reproductive matters enhanced. He will have to go to a clinic to be tested, inspected and sorted out with the right dose and type. He will enter the domain of the Earth Mother. He will go walking on the alien planet Womb. In time, he may even feel he belongs there: they're his hormones, after all. And, of course, when he gets home he'll have to remember to take it. This will be in his own financial interest as well as anything else. The days when a man could make a woman pregnant and make off without a care are gone: the Child Support Agency will be after him if the courts aren't already; public opinion has already been mobilized to disapprove and as 'responsibility' cements its position as a political buzzword in the age of family crisis, that disapproval can only intensify.

The male Pill's effect of facilitating greater equality of control over fertility will, though, also enable men to match women's capacity to abuse that control. Because they will be able to stop taking the Pill without their abstinence being detected, men will be as free to make unprotected women pregnant against their wishes as women are to get themselves pregnant against the wishes of men. There will, of course, be limits to his control over the upshot of such unscrupulousness: after all, the 'egg-napper' won't be able to take his hostage into his body as the 'sperm-napper' does. But an aspect of the new gender near-equality is that men's and women's absolute need for each other will be equally diminished. As a result the man who is desperate for a child and can find no suitable female partner with which to have one will need to despair no more, at least as long as he isn't poor.

The burgeoning market in eggs, wombs and semen which has accompanied the emergence of surrogacy has enabled gay men to become fathers by making arrangements with surrogate mothers. But they won't be the only men without female partners to benefit. The lone male heterosexual parent whose biological son or daughter has been cultivated to order cannot be far away, and may even be with us already. All he'll need do is locate a suitable uterus to let and provide the rent money. And age will be no barrier. The public is still getting over the shock of an Italian woman of sixty having a baby conceived with a younger woman's eggs. A sixty-year-old man will be able to do the same thing with far less inconvenience. Indeed, the prescient twenty-year-old may make plans for such an occurrence. As an insurance against loss of quality through age, he will be able to have his sperm frozen and thawed for use in 2040. Perhaps he'll pick his egg partner from a catalogue. What more fulfilling interest to take up after retirement?

Because the road to reproduction's future is not for lady drivers only, and because the presumption that men lack innate nurturing talents is going to be questioned, the whole issue of men's entitlements and liabilities in relation to children and their creation will inevitably be scrutinized again. At present, all the assessment systems honour the principle that the woman is the pre-eminent carer by dint of nature's design. It applies all the way from conception to the custody of children after their parents' separation. There are plenty of arguments in favour of this, and many, rightly, will surely hold. The celebrated case in Scotland in May 1997 where a husband used the courts to try and prevent his estranged wife from having an abortion because her reasons were inadequate highlighted why the law enshrines the women's right to choose: it is she who faces the operation, she who takes the risks, and because the foetus is inside her body it is hers, not his.

But there are also absurdities which will become less and less anomalous, making further regulation of the whole field of familial legal obligations essential. For example: in Britain a man who donates his sperm in a spirit of friendship to a single woman or a lesbian couple he knows is automatically required by law to help support the resulting child financially until adulthood. And what about the man, single or otherwise, who becomes a father through surrogacy: is it logical that he should have precisely the same right to maintenance from the carrier of his foetus? Of course, it would probably have been agreed that no such money would be accepted. But legally he remains vulnerable, and if rancour should disfigure the relationship later the state can pursue him on behalf of the mother until the day he dies. And how about the man who impregnates his partner against her will, keeps the baby after she leaves him and then invites the state to pursue *her* for money?

The more cases like these which arise, the more the difficulties of creating a new framework will become apparent. Under what circumstances should a biological father *not* be expected to fulfil the usual obligations of a father? And in what circumstances should a non-biological father-figure – such as the man in a gay partnership whose sperm was *not* used to fertilize a surrogate but who wanted the child and paid half the fee – be required to fulfil those same obligations?

Gazing into this mist of the future it is possible to make out two strange masculine shapes.

One is the career sperm donor. If freed of the potential liabilities that presently accrue automatically from having a biological link to a child, a new avenue of opportunity would be opened up for gentleman entrepreneurs as suppliers of high-grade semen. Women, maybe even accompanied by barren male partners, could shop around for the best deal. With sperm counts thought to be falling, high yields would be at a premium. The donor could be selected through an agency, perhaps viewed via a television shopping channel. There might then be a face-to-face interview, a thorough physical inspection and an analysis of a sample of the goods. The reproductive fluid could then be delivered to the customer's door in a sealed, cooled container, ready to serve.

The other is a concept, a tentative intellectual construct – and let us now forgo the pleasures of facetiousness – which redefines the meaning of fatherhood for the child-centred era. No longer would the label 'father' be affixed purely on the evidence of a genetic fingerprint. This would be but one criteria, not necessarily superior to a supportable pledge by another interested adult male of a consistently high level of commitment and care. For, while biology is important, a channel to the soul, it does not guarantee a happy destiny for far too many children. And it seems reasonable at least to speculate that in a future filled with gay marriages, 'blended' step-families and fugitives fleeing from the likes of the CSA, linkage to a child through a bloodline may come to count for less than it does now. And as forward-thinking dads converge with modern mothers towards parental androgyny, the question will be asked again: just what are fathers for?

There is an affirmative answer. No matter how much the once exclusive territories of motherhood and fatherhood merge on the common ground of parenthood, there will probably always be some things which dads provide best, and some that mums do. In his book *The Heart of Parenting*, American psychologist John Gottman dedicates a chapter to 'the father's crucial role'. He wants dads to be full parental partners from pregnancy onwards, but underlines their gender-distinctiveness. For Gottman, men's tendency to be more boisterous with children than women is not just a socially constructed custom but also the psychologically valuable expression of a genetic tendency. 'Imagine dad as a "scary bear" chasing a delighted toddler across the yard,' Gottman writes, 'or lifting and twirling the child over his head for an "airplane ride". Such games allow the child to experience the thrill of being just a little bit scared, but amused and aroused at the same time.'

Genetic explanations for different behavioural proclivities shown by male and female remain hugely contentious – and too specialized an area to be adjudicated on here. However, Gottman's *conclusions* about the benefits of men's behaviour as parents suggest that there will be a separate and valuable space marked 'male' for the foreseeable future. But how will it be filled?

Let's hold our breath.

On the one hand: the spluttering of fuddy-duddies is futile and their deepest fears will be realized. Never again will masculinity be as containable or as easy to describe in false terms as it has been during the last 150 years. Tomorrow's materially comfortable young men will have more freedom of identity on their hands than their grandfathers and even their fathers could have imagined. The luckiest will achieve the state of sustained independence which forebears enjoyed for a few years only before slipping into the state of mind called suburbia. The dawning of the Teen Age, first in America then elsewhere, uncoupled younger men from the long train of precedent. They didn't have to follow in their fathers' footsteps, or be replicas of them in any way. Kids had their own cash to spend, which meant Teen Boys might have their *own* music, their *own* cars, their *own* movies, their *own* nights out. Their own fights, too. And, of course, their own Teen Girls to chase and kiss and fuck in the bushes after fumbling with the prophylactics which the boldest had gone out and bought. But it was liberty on a short-term licence because pre-war standards still ruled. Even in the not-so-swinging Sixties most older men lived in a house with a wife and no other adults except, perhaps, for elderly parents. And however much, and for whatever reasons, some may have hated the idea, most young men, including a lot of those with Beatle haircuts, accepted that this was their destiny too.

In Britain the popular culture reflected the key themes of young British working- and lower-middle-class manhood: frustration and release. They are most famously there in the Rolling Stones' shortage of 'Satisfaction', the Who's stammering eulogizing of 'My Generation', the Beatles' rasping incitement to 'Twist and Shout'. But the tensions and limitations of independence were explored too. In 1960 Albert Finney made a stunning addition to the panoply of movie manhood playing Arthur Seaton in Karel Reisz's film adaptation of Alan Sillitoe's novel *Saturday Night and Sunday Morning*. Seaton is a brash Nottingham factory worker with money in his pocket, a drinker and a womanizer who's decided he will live life as he bloody well pleases. It doesn't last. He impregnates a workmate's wife and finally finds himself contemplating marriage to a lively but conventional girl on a bland new housing estate. The film was striking for its regional realism and for the ambitions of its leading character. Seaton was not content to be in control in the usual masculine way: he wanted to be *out* of control as well.

By contrast Billy Fisher's problem was that he never managed to let go. *Billy Liar* was the protagonist of Keith Waterhouse's comic novel, published in 1959. It was turned into a play and, in 1963, a film directed by John Schlesinger. The adolescent hero (Tom Courtenay) has nothing to stop him leaving his job as an undertaker's dogsbody in a small town in Yorkshire and heading for London's gilded flagstones. Nothing, that is, except his own lack of nerve. He comes close to making his escape. He even buys a train ticket. But in the end he prefers the smothering, fractious security of his parents' home and his private fantasy world in which he is the hero, a conquering general, ruler of all.

However, another young character in the story does start the journey: Billy's free-wheeling, button-bright, blonde-haired sometime girlfriend Liz (Julie Christie). Tomorrow's young men would not have thought twice about getting on the train with her. And they would have been careful not to get trapped like Arthur Seaton (they'd probably have all been on the future Pill). Unlike Billy's and Arthur's, their lifestyle options will multiply. They will be free to live in ways which would have been frowned upon or even outlawed in the past. If they don't want to 'settle down' into a heterosexual union almost before they are shaving regularly, there will be far fewer pressures on them to do it, and if a heterosexual union is the last kind they'd ever join they will be far less obliged to keep it a disfiguring little secret. Instead, they may decide to travel for a while, to live alone, to live in companionable squalor among a bunch of fellow men until deep into their twenties, or to build with one other man a cosy nest for homosexual cohabitation. They will learn about housekeeping as well as goalkeeping. They will discover that the term 'white goods' is not the new shorthand for stuff you scrape into lines and shove up your nose.

More men will remain economically unencumbered for longer, living for more of their lives in childless households. In Britain in 1968, 66 per cent of men aged between twenty-five and thirty-four lived in households with children. By 1993 that fraction had fallen to 40 per cent. It will go on falling, and because they will routinely expect to live to a hundred those young men won't be in a rush. They will be lucky, and it will be wrong to begrudge them their luck. The best efforts of parents, politicians, trade unionists, educators and others have gone into creating a pool of luck from which they may draw. And many will make their own luck. We should be glad they will be rid of the burdens their fathers and grandfathers had to carry.

Even present-day first impressions hint at how much more relaxed and elastic the category of masculinity is becoming: men do not look alike any more. Looks aren't everything, as every sensible girl knows. But the adventurousness of the male wardrobe is astonishing compared with fifty years ago. The appearances of the earliest post-war men varied significantly only according to class and occupation, but today men's outward multifariousness is kaleidoscopic. It can be deceptive, too. Once, a man's rig was a reliable mirror of his status, but now he makes eloquent sartorial statements to the world which may reveal more about how he would like to be perceived than about who he actually is. Often the statement is muted, but a stiff shirt collar displayed over the neck of a casual sweater is a statement nonetheless. Sometimes the statement is ostentatiously individual, augmented with scented armpits and an elaborate coiffure. A man may be poor but dressing up; he may be rich but dressing down. He may be white and aspiring to blackness. He may be gay pretending to be straight or – more likely these days – the other way round. The fellow in the tweed jacket with leather elbow-patches might be Tristan from Oxford or Kev from the East End.

All this says as much about the widening reach of consumer capitalism – the seductiveness of marketing messages like the one which convinced men it was all right to wear perfume if they could call it aftershave – as it does about the way men really are and will be. But it still serves as an example and a telling metaphor, each illuminating the extent to which a man can already pick an identity off the peg. The choices will be far from unlimited or available to all. But they undoubtedly will exist. Men have always strayed from the masculine mean, but not always very freely. In the future there will be a lot of new and better ways of being male.

On the other hand: a lot of men will go crazy. Some will not know or give a damn about anything but themselves. Others will just stay trapped in an empty inner space, like the one Alan Bleasdale invented for Yosser Hughes in the elegiac yet prescient *Boys from the Blackstuff*, or the one Joseph Heller explored in *Something Happened*, a brilliant, terrible novel in which almost nothing happens at all. The future of such men is to be locked into a kind of evolutionary limbo, unwilling or unable to make constructive use of new possibilities. They will retreat yet more deeply into their habitual spiritual solitariness and the barren nihilism which so often flourishes there. There will be no lack of incentives for them to work more obsessively, to lie, cheat and destroy more ruthlessly or to give less of a damn than ever about those around them. There will be more reason for them to take excessive refuge in the gloomy citadels of self-pity. They will race down the road to ruin alone, blinded by empty ambitions, worry and incoherent rage. They will go absolutely nowhere except the hangdog refuge of yesterday's discredited myths. They will go on killing themselves at a terrifying rate.

Not all will find the traps closing around them. But even those who don't may fail to resemble the New Model Male which society urgently needs. It is already established that younger men's responses to the constant reality of job insecurity is to accept it and live for the moment, spending money while they have it, gobbling up all the short-term self-gratification they can eat. It is easy to see the logic of this. Easy to envy it, too. Yet it also raises the depressing prospect of an entire male social stratum who see adult life as an extended state of adolescence (and Robert Bly may be on to something there). The capacity of young and not-so-young men, including those who are highly educated and with considerable professional responsibilities, to remain puerile far into adulthood is already a depressing feature of contemporary life.

Some will simply shrug and say that men were ever thus, just as they were ever philanderers and fatheads. But even if that is so, at least those who remained juvenile beyond their years in the past were only doing what was socially ordained. Today, by contrast, it has become a lifestyle option. The advance of male immaturity is apparent everywhere, in the dreary 'post-ironic' prurience of men's style magazine (many of them bought by forty-ish professionals), in the sale of replica football shirts to full grown adults. Gay men too can make eternal boyhood their consumer choice. Hence, the gay columnist Paul Burston attacking gay lifestyle conformists: 'See them wherever there is a pose to be struck and a few pink pounds to be squandered. Watch them as they go about their daily routine of primping, preening and perking their tits up at the gym. Study them closely, and you'll be forced to agree that our booming "Gay" scene has spawned a generation of Stepford Boys'.

There is a pressing need for the parameters, components and qualities required of a better future manhood to be articulated as convincingly and with the same capacity to inspire as those praised by conservatives when they hark back to their ideal pasts. Yet there is not much sign of this need being met. Part of the problem is that men who've acknowledged the historical shortcomings of their sex feel nervous of expressing solutions publicly, whether among friends in the pub or in the pages of posh newspapers. Such men make themselves vulnerable to attack from many quarters, ranging from fellow men unnerved by their pertinence (or impertinence) to the more territorial kind of (female) feminist who insists that such critiques are driven by obsequious ulterior motives. Mockery is always just around the corner. New Man may have only been a piece of adland shorthand, but did that make him a bad guy?

Another reason it has been difficult for men to engage constructively with the gender debate is that its terms have so often been defined by those with an interest in rendering it facile. Set piece media battles in the 'war of the sexes' may inflame passions but are a soft-headed way of handling the subject when the underlying trend is for the social divisions between men and women to break down and blur rather than harden. Emphasising this is not the same thing as anticipating – or advocating – a complete dissolution. Yes, it is possible to imagine a future in which the differences between men and women will be so negligible as to be barely worth considering. But such a future is so far off that it makes the distinction between rational prediction and sheer speculation equally meaningless. And even those who come down strongly on the nurture side of the (generally fatuous) 'nature-nurture' argument, find it hard to disagree with the proposition that for as long as two sexes exist, all women will have physical and emotional experiences in common which all men will be unable to fully share – and vice versa. Yet the evidence of ongoing convergence is equally obvious. Men can either be fools and try to fight it or they can be wise and welcome it. The key issue for the future of men should not be how to win the 'sex war', but how best to secure the peace.

This will involve men and women alike accommodating more flexible models of masculinity which acknowledge many features in common with femininity and which, largely as a result of this, are also able to accommodate those aspects of 'masculinity' which do not do damage to children or women and do not denigrate either those men who do not exhibit the same 'masculine' traits or those women who do. In this process men will be under the greater pressure to change, for they will need to share pieces of male territory with women with better grace than they have sometimes exhibited before. This need not mean men having to grudgingly forego all the things about being men which have been pleasurable or distinctive. Neither does it require them to make frenzied acquaintance with their suppressed 'feminine' inner selves, leading to therapist couches being monopolized by balding bankers and brawny bricklayers bemoaning their testosterone and filling the waste bins with sodden mansize tissues.

Plenty of human virtues conventionally associated with men are well worth celebrating: adventurousness, physical courage, risk-taking, rugged individualism. Withdrawing from the 'sex war' is not all about guilt, sacrifice or endless demonstrations of painful sensitivity. It is largely a matter of plain common sense at a time when ever greater numbers of men swell the ranks of society's walking wounded. As Phillip Hodson has written: 'If men as a sex were quoted on the stock exchange, nobody would buy the shares. At every level of education men are increasingly out-performed by women. Men lack the cooperative, intuitive skills required in the future team-working world. We are more prone to stress and illness in everyday life ... in every sense of the word *modern men don't work.*'

The situation is *serious*. And any truly new man for the new century needs to be a *serious* man if he is going to seize the opportunity to get himself and his fellow men out of it. That does not mean, as so many sons (and daughters) of the Eighties seem to think, that he would therefore be a drab and humourless man. He should be anything but either. The point is that his colourfulness and humour would be aspects of his seriousness, not evidence of its absence. He would be interested in and by almost everything around him, and he would be the more entertained by the world he moved in, and other worlds beyond, *because* his seriousness enabled him to understand it more fully.

Most seriously of all, men must strive to understand themselves and what has made them what they are from the earliest years of their lives. Only then will men be able to embark on perhaps the most crucial task of all – improving the future of boys. It is during boyhood that

53

the iron laws of masculine orthodoxy are most repressively imposed, and all the more effectively because a boy has had so little time to understand those laws, still less to challenge their validity. At the age of around seven, any reasonably happy, well-adjusted boy is a creature who brims with joy. He still wants and needs to cuddle up with his parents. But he is also stepping into the next phase of growing up, adventuring deeper into the world, finding out about being with friends of his own sex. He enjoys the company of the group, the feeling of belonging, his growing acquaintance with his own powers and the independence they bestow. Whatever it is he likes to do best, he just cannot get enough. He oozes enthusiasm, tenderness and trust, and his every small accomplishment fills his father with pride.

Yet, even if only unconsciously, that father knows something very tragic that, as yet, his son does not. He knows that all this joy is going to be ended in around three years' time when the son will have to learn what is required of him by peers of both sexes if he is to be accepted as a man. He will be expected to taunt or be taunted, bully or be bullied, destroy or be destroyed. He will be expected to conform to the codes of the male group or be ruthlessly excluded from it. He will be expected to conceal or strip away any semblance of sensitivity or sympathy for others who are excluded, taunted, bullied and destroyed. A dislike of cruelty will be mocked. His sexuality will be tested, and he will be harshly punished if any hint of what might be construed as a homosexual leaning is identified. And, of course, he will be expected to have no emotional contact with girls. Sexual contact, yes, in time, and of the most coarse and unfeeling kind. But no emotional contact. No emotions, if possible, at all.

The little boy's father knows this as he watches him leave infanthood behind. He knows he has to prepare him for what is to come. There are two ways to make this preparation: by accepting the rules of the game, and so perpetuating it; or by teaching his son that there is a better way of being male. There is a sense in which the future of men was started by women. Now men must do some of the work. They should begin at the beginning: with themselves and with their sons.

Further Reading

Bly, Robert, *Iron John* (Element, 1990)

Bly, Robert, *The Sibling Society* (Penguin, 1996)

Burgess, Adrienne, *Fatherhood Reclaimed* (Vermilion, 1997)

Burgess, Adrienne and Ruxton, Sandy, *Men and their Children* (IPPR, 1996)

Burston, Paul, *What Are You Looking At?* (Cassell, 1995)

Cadbury, Deborah, *The Feminisation of Nature* (Hamish Hamilton, 1997)

Cooper, Mick and Baker, Peter, *The MANual* (Thorsons, 1996)

Davenport-Hines, Richard, *Sex, Death and Punishment* (Collins, 1990)

Gottman, John, *The Heart of Parenting* (Bloomsbury, 1997)

Hargreaves, John, *Sport, Power and Culture* (Polity, 1986)

Hite, Shere, *The Hite Report on the Family* (Sceptre, 1994)

Hite, Shere, *The Hite Report on Men and Male Sexuality* (Vermillion, 1990)

Howarth, Peter, *Fatherhood* (Gollancz, 1997)

Simpson, Mark, *It's a Queer World* (Vintage, 1996)

Smith, Joan, *Misogynies* (Vintage, 1996)

Stevenson, John, *British Society 1914–45* (Penguin; 1984)

Sullivan, Andrew, *Virtually Normal* (Picador, 1995)

Willis, Paul, *Common Culture* (Oxford University Press, 1990)

PREDICTIONS